SEMITE VS SEMITE

MAYAR AKASH

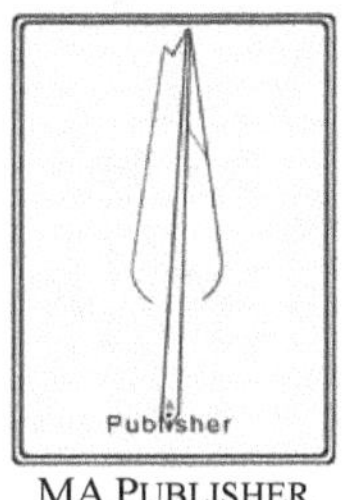

MA PUBLISHER

Produced by Mayar Akash

Published by MA Publishing (Penzance)
Email: mapublisher@yahoo.com
Released on Sept 2025

Printed in the UK,
14 Adelaide Street, Penzance, TR18 2ER

ISBN-13: 978-1-915958280

Disclaimer:
The content of the book has been compiled through a series of questions and prompts with "Copilot" 2025.

Cover designed by Mayar Akash
Typeset in Times Roman

Paper printed on is FSC Certified, lead free, acid free, buffered paper made from wood-based pulp. Our paper meets the ISO 9706 standard for permanent paper. As such, paper will last several hundred years when stored.

Dedication

For the ones who remember what was lost
For the ones who carry their keys in exile
For the children who sleep beneath drones
For the elders who whisper history through locked doors
For every name that was erased but never forgotten

This book is for Palestine.
Its breath. Its soil. Its truth.

And for those who refuse to look away.

Acknowledgement

To the steadfast hands that shaped my voice—
Thank you to my parents, whose stories stitched the fabric of my consciousness, and whose resilience is etched into every page.
To my siblings, for the laughter that softened the weight of memory.
To the friends who read drafts, shared coffee, and reminded me that stories are a shared inheritance.
To the educators and elders who taught me that history isn't in books alone—it lives in breath, in dirt, in defiance.

To Palestine: this book is a small offering in the mosaic of our truth.
To those who walk with grief in their pockets, and hope tucked inside it.

And to the reader—thank you for holding this story.

Content

Foreword

Why Truth Must Speak

"This book is not written for comfort. It is written for clarity. It is written for those who refuse to be paralyzed by propaganda, and who believe that history must be reclaimed by the dispossessed."

In a world where silence is rewarded and complicity is normalized, Mayar's work is a rupture. It is a refusal to forget. It is a challenge to every institution that has turned its back on Palestine — from governments to universities, from media outlets to religious bodies.

This book is not anti-Jewish. It is anti-erasure. It is anti-colonial. It is a call to conscience from one Semitic people to another — and to the world that has watched one Semitic group brutalize another with impunity.

Mayar's voice is not just a voice of resistance. It is a voice of reclamation. It is a voice that demands we remember what was done, what is being done, and what must never be allowed again.

Preface

There are stories we inherit like scars—quiet, deep, and undeniable.
This book began not as a declaration, but as a reckoning.

In fragments, I chased the voices of a silenced history. In dust, I found defiant breath. These pages are stitched with longing, inscribed with the echo of homes shuttered and hearts unrelenting.
I did not write it to convince. I wrote it because silence is a kind of death.

Here you'll find no neat endings. Just truth pressed between sentences, and the question: what does it mean to remember?

May this book be a witness.

Chapter Breakdown & Historical Timeline

1. Introduction: The Semitic Paradox

- Define "Semitic" linguistically and ethnically.
- Explore the irony of Semitic-on-Semitic violence.
- Introduce your thesis: historical truth vs. modern paralysis.

2. Ancient Roots: Pre-Roman Palestine

- Indigenous populations: Canaanites, Philistines, Hebrews.
- Early Semitic tribes and their coexistence.
- Clarify that original Palestinians were not Muslims—many were pagans, Christians, and Jews.

3. Roman Conquest & Judea (63 BCE onward)

- Pompey's invasion and the end of Hasmonean independence.
- Roman administrative control and the rise of client kings.
- Herod the Great: an Idumean Arab appointed "King of the Jews".

4. The Herodian Dynasty

- Herod's rule, alliances with Rome, and brutal legacy.
- Religious and ethnic tensions under Herodian rule.
- Herod's successors and the fragmentation of Judea.

5. The Flavian Dynasty & the Jewish-Roman Wars

- Vespasian and Titus: suppression of Jewish revolts.
- Destruction of the Second Temple (70 CE).
- Renaming of Judea to *Syria Palaestina* by Hadrian after the Bar Kokhba revolt (135 CE).

Note: The name "Palestine" was not derived from "Flavian" but from "Philistia," referencing the ancient Philistines. Romans used "Palestina" to erase Jewish identity after the revolt.

6. Byzantine & Islamic Transitions

- Byzantine Christian rule and Jewish marginalization.
- Early Islamic conquest (7th century): Arabs rename the region *Filastin.*
- Coexistence of Jews, Christians, and Muslims under various caliphates.

7. Ottoman Era & British Mandate

- Ottoman administration (1517–1917): multi-faith society.
- British Mandate: rise of nationalism, Jewish immigration, and Arab resistance.

8. Mythmaking & Identity Politics

- Debunk myths: "Palestinians are recent migrants," "Palestine never existed," etc..
- Clarify that "Palestinian" identity evolved politically but has deep cultural and geographic roots.
- Address misuse of history to delegitimize indigenous claims.

9. Modern Conflict: Semitic vs. Semitic

- Zionism and its impact on Arab Jews and Palestinians.
- The paradox of Jewish statehood displacing other Semitic peoples.
- The psychological and geopolitical paralysis of the global community.

10. Conclusion: Truth as Resistance

- Reclaiming historical nuance.
- Calling for moral clarity and solidarity.
- Position your book as a tool for awakening and justice.

Introduction

The Semitic Paradox

"What is more tragic than brother against brother? When the blood spilled is not from strangers, but from kin—linked by ancestry, yet divided by myth."

The Irony of Shared Ancestry

Jews and Palestinians share deep Semitic roots, linguistically and ethnically. Both trace origins to ancient peoples of the Levant: Aramaic-speaking tribes, Canaanites, Hebrews, and Philistines. The term "Semitic" itself comes from Shem, one of Noah's sons, and encompasses a group of languages (Hebrew, Arabic, Aramaic) and cultures that evolved together across centuries.

To witness one Semitic group systematically disenfranchise, occupy, and kill another is not just a political tragedy—it's a profound betrayal of historical kinship.

Palestine Before Islam

Before the rise of Islam in the 7th century, Palestine was home to:

- Pagan Canaanite and Philistine communities.
- Ancient Hebrews.
- Nabateans, Samaritans, and early Christians. Many of these groups were indigenous to the region long before

monotheism transformed the spiritual landscape. The label “Palestinian” didn’t originally denote religion—it denoted land, culture, and ancestry.

The Myth of Palestinian Non-Existence

- Claiming Palestinians are recent migrants ignores Byzantine and Islamic records referring to the local *Filastin* province.
- Romans themselves renamed Judea to *Syria Palaestina* in 135 CE—a move not to honor Philistines, but to punish and erase Jewish rebellion.

Crucial Clarification: The term *Palestine* was **not** derived from "Flavian." The Flavian dynasty (Vespasian, Titus) was involved in crushing the Jewish revolt and destroying the Second Temple, but it was Emperor Hadrian (from the later Nerva-Antonine dynasty) who renamed the region to “Palestina.” The name was borrowed from the coastal Philistine tribes—not the ruling Roman family.

A Beacon of Truth

This book is not anti-Jewish. It is anti-historical erasure and anti-occupation. It aims to reclaim a shared narrative rooted in truth, not twisted by nationalism, colonial framing, or divine entitlement.

“History is not what happened. It is what we choose to remember—and what we choose to forget.”

Prologue

Nakba, 1948.

The year the map tore, and the land swallowed its name.

It did not begin with war—it began with doors locked behind fleeing hands, with stories stuffed into satchels alongside keys and deeds. It began with my grandmother's silence and the way she folded her grief into bread. The world called it a conflict. We called it a catastrophe.

I inherited the echo of that moment not through dates, but through absence. No photos remain of the orange groves. No recordings of the songs they hummed while planting. Only shadows passed down in stories we weren't supposed to tell.

This book rises from the rubble of 1948, not to explain, but to remember. Each chapter is a return—to a porch never rebuilt, a fig tree never replanted, a name never reprinted.

Because to write is to reclaim.
And to remember is to resist.

Chapter 1

The Semitic Paradox

The DNA of Shared Identity

The irony is staggering: a people descended from common ancestors, speaking related languages, shaped by the same desert winds and tribal customs—are locked in conflict so deep, the world forgets they were once indistinguishable. Hebrew and Arabic are linguistic cousins, echoing the rhythms of ancient Aramaic and Canaanite tongues. To declare that one Semitic people is more entitled to land than another is to ignore thousands of years of tangled heritage.

Semitic, by definition, includes:

- **Jews**, **Arabs**, **Assyrians**, and **Arameans**.
- Languages like **Hebrew**, **Arabic**, **Amharic**, and **Aramaic**.
- Peoples bound not by religion, but by historical migration and linguistic evolution across Mesopotamia, the Levant, and the Arabian Peninsula.

A False Dichotomy

Modern discourse often pits "Jews" vs. "Palestinians" as polar opposites. But look deeper:

- Many Palestinian families have Jewish ancestry, converted over centuries.
- Arab Jews existed across the Middle East, from Morocco to Baghdad.
- Ethnic purity is a myth. Identity, especially Semitic identity, is fluid—shaped by empire, theology, survival.

To simplify the conflict to **Jews vs. Muslims** is to erase:

- The **Christian Palestinians** who predated Islamic rule.
- The **Jewish Palestinians** who lived under Ottoman and Arab control.
- The **multi-faith, multi-ethnic coexistence** that marked earlier centuries.

From Shared Wounds to Erased Histories

The trauma of the Holocaust birthed Zionism's urgency. But in doing so, it sidelined other Semitic narratives:

- **Nakba** (1948 Palestinian displacement) remains unacknowledged in many Jewish histories.
- Arab Jews were uprooted from their homelands post-1948—not to find peace, but often discrimination within Israel.
- The global paralysis stems not from ignorance, but discomfort: acknowledging Palestinian suffering would mean admitting that moral clarity isn't always one-sided.

Moral Disintegration

- Killing kin is not just war—it's spiritual decay.
- Occupation becomes possible only when one forgets their shared reflection.
- Israel's current policies do not represent all Jews—many resist what they see as betrayal of Jewish ethics.

"A Semitic war is not a war of enemies. It is a war of the mirror—where each strike wounds the self."

Chapter 2

Ancient Roots—Pre-Roman Palestine

The Land Before Labels

Long before the Roman boot crushed the soil of Judea, Palestine was a crossroads of civilizations. It wasn't a monolith—it was a living, breathing tapestry of tribes, languages, and spiritual traditions. The people who lived here weren't "Palestinians" in the modern sense, but they were undeniably indigenous to the land.

- **Canaanites**: The earliest known inhabitants, thriving from ~3000 BCE.
- **Philistines**: Arrived around 1175 BCE, likely from the Aegean, settled in coastal cities like Gaza, Ashkelon, and Ekron.
- **Hebrews**: Semitic tribes who emerged in the highlands, eventually forming Israel and Judah.
- **Arameans, Edomites, Moabites, Ammonites**: Neighboring Semitic peoples with shared cultural and linguistic roots.

These groups didn't live in isolation—they traded, intermarried, fought, and worshipped side by side.

Languages of the Land

Palestine was a linguistic borderland, shaped by empire and migration.

- **Canaanite dialects**: Early Semitic tongues spoken by indigenous tribes.

- **Hebrew**: Emerged from Canaanite roots, used by Israelites.
- **Aramaic**: Became dominant in daily life by the Roman period.
- **Greek**: Introduced via Hellenistic influence, later used in administration and Christian texts.

"To speak in Palestine was to echo the tongues of gods, traders, and rebels."

Spiritual Diversity & Beliefs

Before monotheism took hold, Palestine was spiritually pluralistic.

- **Polytheism & Henotheism**: Worship of multiple gods, often with one supreme deity (El, Baal, Yahweh).
- **Divine Council**: Belief in a pantheon of gods governing nature and fate.
- **Local Deities**: Each region had its own patron gods—Yahweh in the highlands, Baal in Phoenicia, Chemosh in Moab.

Religious beliefs in Judea were **not radically different** from those in neighboring regions like Damascus, Ugarit, or Ammon. The idea of spiritual exclusivity came much later.

Genetic Continuity & Indigenous Identity

Modern genetic studies show that Palestinians today share deep ancestry with Bronze Age Levantines.

- **Canaanite-like DNA**: Found in both Palestinians and Jews.
- **Cultural continuity**: Despite conquests, the local population remained largely intact.
- **Religious shifts**: Pagan, Jewish, Christian, and Muslim identities layered over the same ancestral roots.

"To be Palestinian is not just to be Arab or Muslim—it is to carry the memory of Canaan in your blood."

Debunking Myths

Let's start dismantling the falsehoods:

- ❌"Palestinians are recent migrants."
  ✅Archaeology and genetics show continuous habitation for thousands of years.
- ❌"Philistines were barbaric invaders."
  ✅They were advanced, seafaring people who assimilated and contributed to local culture.
- ❌"Palestine was empty before Zionism."
  ✅The land was densely populated with diverse communities long before the 20th century.

Chapter 3

Rome's Grip Tightens—From Herod to Imperial Rule

The Roman Conquest of Judea (63 BCE)

- In 63 BCE, Roman general **Pompey** invaded Jerusalem during a Hasmonean civil war between **Hyrcanus II** and **Aristobulus II**.
- Pompey installed Hyrcanus II as High Priest but denied him kingship, effectively ending Hasmonean independence.
- Judea became a **Roman client state**, ruled indirectly through local elites.

"Rome didn't conquer Judea with swords alone—it conquered it with bureaucracy, betrayal, and the illusion of autonomy."

Herod the Great: Rome's Loyal Tyrant

- Herod, an **Idumean Arab** by descent, was appointed **King of the Jews** by the Roman Senate in 40 BCE.
- He seized power in 37 BCE after defeating Antigonus II with Roman military support.
- Though he rebuilt the **Second Temple** and launched massive infrastructure projects, Herod was seen by many Jews as a **foreign puppet**.

Herod's Contradictions:

Trait	Reality
Ethnicity	Arab (Idumean) and Nabatean roots
Religion	Practiced Judaism, but not accepted as Jewish by many
Loyalty	Fiercely loyal to Rome, not to Jewish autonomy
Legacy	Builder of cities, destroyer of dynasties

- Herod executed **Mariamne I**, his Hasmonean wife, and their sons, fearing rebellion.
- His rule was marked by **paranoia, brutality**, and **political brilliance**.

The Herodian Tetrarchy & Roman Annexation

- After Herod's death in 4 BCE, his kingdom was divided among his sons:
    - **Herod Archelaus** ruled Judea, Samaria, and Idumea.
    - **Herod Antipas** governed Galilee and Perea.
    - **Philip the Tetrarch** controlled the northeastern territories.
- Archelaus was so brutal and incompetent that Rome **deposed him in 6 CE**, annexing Judea as a **Roman province**.
- This marked the end of local rule and the beginning of **direct Roman administration**.

Seeds of Revolt

- Roman governors (like **Pontius Pilate**) imposed taxes, desecrated sacred sites, and ruled with cruelty.
- Jewish resistance grew: **Zealots**, **Sicarii**, and **messianic movements** began to form.
- The stage was set for the **First Jewish-Roman War** (66–73 CE).

"Herod's throne was built on Roman stone—but its foundation was cracked by betrayal."

Chapter 4

The Flavian Suppression—Erasure by Empire

The Jewish-Roman War (66–73 CE)

- Sparked by Roman brutality, taxation, and desecration of sacred spaces.
- Jewish factions—Zealots, Sicarii, and others—rose in revolt.
- The war escalated into a full-scale rebellion, with Jerusalem as its epicenter.

"Rome didn't just crush a rebellion—it crushed a memory."

The Flavian Dynasty: Vespasian, Titus, Domitian

Emperor	Role in Suppression	Legacy
Vespasian	Led initial campaign; became emperor during war	Used victory to legitimize Flavian rule
Titus	Besieged and destroyed Jerusalem in 70 CE	Oversaw destruction of Second Temple
Domitian	Continued anti-Jewish policies	Enforced Jewish tax and imperial propaganda

- The **siege of Jerusalem** was brutal: starvation, infighting, and mass slaughter.
- **Second Temple destroyed**—a spiritual and cultural catastrophe.

- **Masada** fell in 73 CE after mass suicide by Jewish rebels.

Erasure Through Renaming

After the **Bar Kokhba Revolt** (132–135 CE), Emperor **Hadrian** renamed:

- **Judea → Syria Palaestina**
- Aimed to **erase Jewish identity** from the land

Important Clarification: The name *Palestine* was **not** derived from the Flavian dynasty.
It was borrowed from the ancient **Philistines**, and had been used by **Greek writers like Herodotus** centuries earlier.

- Romans used the name as a **punitive measure** to sever Jewish ties to the land.
- This act of imperial rebranding was **unique**— no other Roman province was renamed in this way following rebellion.

Psychological Warfare & Propaganda

- **Triumphal arches**, coins, and literature glorified the Flavian victory.
- **Josephus**, a Jewish historian turned Roman client, wrote *The Jewish War* to justify Roman actions.
- The Flavians used the war to **legitimize their dynasty**, portraying Jews as dangerous rebels.

"The Flavian dynasty didn't just win a war—they rewrote the story of who belonged."

Debunking Myths

- ❌"Palestine was invented by Romans."
  ✅The name existed long before—used by Egyptians, Assyrians, Greeks.
- ❌"Palestinians are not indigenous."
  ✅The people of the land—Canaanites, Philistines, Hebrews—share deep ancestral ties to modern Palestinians.
- ❌"Judea and Palestine were separate."
  ✅They were overlapping terms used by different empires at different times.

Chapter 5

Faith and Flux—Byzantine to Islamic Palestine

Byzantine Rule (4th–7th Century CE)

After Rome's Christianization, Palestine became a spiritual epicenter:

- **Constantine the Great** commissioned churches like the Church of the Holy Sepulchre.
- **Palaestina Prima, Secunda, and Salutaris** were administrative provinces under Byzantine control.
- Christianity flourished, but **Jews were marginalized**, and **Samaritans faced suppression.**

Religious Landscape:

Faith Group	Status under Byzantines
Christians	Dominant, state religion
Jews	Marginalized, taxed, restricted
Samaritans	Suppressed after revolts
Pagans	Declined, often persecuted

"The land was holy—but holiness was weaponized."

The Persian Interlude (614–628 CE)

- In 614, a **joint Sasanian-Jewish army** briefly captured Jerusalem.
- Jews hoped for restoration, but Persians withdrew, and Byzantines retaliated.
- **Nehemiah ben Hushiel**, a Jewish leader, was executed; Jewish hopes were crushed.

Islamic Conquest (634–638 CE)

- Led by **Caliph Umar ibn al-Khattab**, Muslim forces defeated Byzantines at **Yarmouk**.
- Jerusalem surrendered peacefully to Umar in 637.
- Palestine was divided into **Jund Filastin** and **Jund al-Urdunn**, military districts under the **Rashidun Caliphate**.

Key Transitions:

Empire	Capital	Religious Policy
Byzantines	Constantinople	Christian supremacy
Rashidun Caliphate	Medina	Dhimmi system: protected status for Jews & Christians

Jund Filastin: Governance & Coexistence

- Capital shifted from **Jerusalem** to **Ramla**.
- **Christians, Jews, and Muslims** coexisted under **dhimmi law**: protected but taxed.
- Arabic gradually replaced Greek and Aramaic as the **lingua franca**.

"Islam didn't erase Palestine's past—it layered it."

Coexistence Before Zionism

- Arab Jews, Christians, and Muslims lived side by side for centuries.
- Shared marketplaces, festivals, and neighborhoods were common.
- **Dhimmi law**, while hierarchical, allowed cultural autonomy and religious freedom.

Debunking Myths

- ❌"Islam erased Jewish and Christian presence."
  ✅Both communities thrived under early Islamic rule.
- ❌"Palestine was always Muslim."
  ✅It was a multi-faith land for centuries, with deep Christian and Jewish roots.
- ❌"Arabic replaced indigenous languages overnight."
  ✅Arabization was gradual, often driven by trade, governance, and cultural exchange.

Chapter 6

Borders and Betrayal—Ottoman Decline to British Mandate

The Ottoman Twilight (1517–1917)

For 400 years, Palestine was part of the Ottoman Empire—a multi-ethnic, multi-faith realm that, despite its flaws, allowed relative coexistence.

- **Tanzimat Reforms (1839–1876)**: Modernization efforts introduced land registration, secular schools, and new administrative centers like **Tulkarm**.
- **Land Code of 1858**: Required peasants to register land, often resulting in loss of ownership due to illiteracy or fear of taxation.
- **Foreign Ownership Laws (1867)**: Allowed non-Ottomans—like Russian Jews—to buy land, laying groundwork for Zionist settlement.

"The empire didn't collapse overnight—it was hollowed out by reform, debt, and betrayal."

Rise of Nationalism & Fragmentation

- Arab intellectuals began advocating for **Ottoman decentralization**, not independence.
- The **Nahda (Arab Renaissance)** fostered secular, multi-faith nationalism—Muslims, Christians, and Jews united under Arab identity.

- But Ottoman repression—especially of Armenians and Arab nationalists—revealed the limits of imperial tolerance.

World War I & Imperial Carve-Up

- Britain made **conflicting promises**:
- **McMahon–Hussein Correspondence (1915)**: Promised Arabs independence.
- **Sykes–Picot Agreement (1916)**: Secretly divided the region with France.
- **Balfour Declaration (1917)**: Supported a Jewish homeland in Palestine.

"Palestine was promised to three powers—none of them Palestinian."

British Mandate (1920–1948)

- Britain took control under the **League of Nations Mandate**, tasked with preparing Palestine for independence.
- Instead, they facilitated **Zionist immigration**, land purchases, and political dominance.
- Palestinian Arabs—who were the majority—were denied self-rule and marginalized.

Key Events:

Year	Event
1920	British Mandate begins; Arab protests erupt
1922	White Paper limits Jewish immigration—but not effectively

Year	Event
1936–1939	Arab Revolt crushed by British forces
1947	UN proposes partition; civil war begins
1948	Mandate ends; **Nakba** begins

Debunking Myths

- ❌"Palestine was a barren land."
  ✅It had thriving cities, agriculture, and a multi-faith population.
- ❌"Zionist immigration was peaceful."
  ✅It displaced thousands of Palestinians and sparked revolts.
- ❌"Britain was a neutral administrator."
  ✅Britain actively favored Zionist goals over indigenous rights.

Chapter 7

The Nakba—Birth of Israel, Death of Palestine

The UN Partition Plan (1947)

- Proposed division: **55% to Jews**, **45% to Arabs**, despite Jews being only ~33% of the population.
- Jerusalem to be internationalized.
- **Zionist leadership accepted**; **Arab leadership rejected**, citing injustice and lack of consultation.

"Palestinians were not asked to give up their land. They were told."

War & Expulsion (1947–1949)

- Zionist militias (Haganah, Irgun, Lehi) launched **Plan Dalet**: aimed to secure territory and remove resistance.
- **Massacres** like **Deir Yassin** (April 1948) triggered panic and mass flight.
- **750,000+ Palestinians** expelled or fled.
- **530 villages destroyed**, names Hebraized, wells poisoned.

Key Events:

Date	Event
Nov 1947	UN Partition Plan adopted
Apr 1948	Deir Yassin massacre
May 14, 1948	Israel declares independence
May 15, 1948	Arab armies invade
1949	Armistice signed; Israel controls 78% of Palestine

The Nakba: Catastrophe in Numbers

- **15,000 Palestinians killed**, mostly civilians.
- **750,000+ displaced**, many still refugees today.
- **400–600 villages erased** from the map.
- **Property seized** under Absentee Property Laws.
- **Law of Return** granted Jews global citizenship rights—**Palestinians denied return**.

"The right of return was not lost. It was stolen."

Psychological Rupture

- Palestinians became stateless, scattered across camps in Lebanon, Syria, Jordan, Gaza, and the West Bank.
- Families separated, identities fragmented.
- The trauma of exile became generational.

"To be Palestinian is to inherit exile."

Debunking Myths

- ❌"Palestinians left voluntarily."
  ✅Most fled under threat, violence, or direct expulsion.
- ❌"Israel was attacked by five armies."
  ✅Arab forces were disorganized; Zionist militias were better equipped and trained.
  - ❌"There was no Palestine."
  ✅Palestine had cities, schools, newspapers, and a rich cultural life before 1948.

Chapter 8

Exile and Resistance—The Rebirth of Palestinian Identity

From Displacement to Defiance

After the Nakba, Palestinians were scattered across refugee camps, cities, and continents. But exile didn't erase identity—it sharpened it.

- **Refugee camps** became crucibles of memory and resistance.
- **Diaspora communities** in Lebanon, Syria, Jordan, and beyond preserved culture through oral history, embroidery, and education.
- **UNRWA schools** educated generations of Palestinians, fostering political awareness and pride.

"We were born everywhere but our own land. We hold every passport but our own."

The Rise of Palestinian Nationalism

- In 1964, the **Palestine Liberation Organization (PLO)** was formed to unify Palestinian factions.
- **Yasser Arafat's Fatah** became the dominant force, advocating armed struggle and political representation.
- The PLO was recognized by the **Arab League (1974)** and gained **UN observer status (1974)**.

Key Milestones:

Year	Event
1964	PLO founded in Jerusalem
1967	Six-Day War intensifies displacement
1974	PLO gains Arab League & UN recognition
1988	PLO accepts UN Resolution 242, recognizes Israel
1993	Oslo Accords: PLO and Israel exchange recognition

Literature as Resistance

Palestinian writers turned trauma into art, memory into defiance.

- **Mahmoud Darwish**: Poet of exile, identity, and resistance.
- **Ghassan Kanafani**: Novelist and martyr, assassinated by Mossad in 1972.
- **Fadwa Tuqan**, **Samih al-Qasim**, **Susan Abulhawa**, **Ghada Karmi**: Voices of longing, rage, and hope.

"To write is to resist. To remember is to reclaim."

Palestinian literature became a **repository of memory**, a **challenge to erasure**, and a **call to justice**.

Cultural Continuity

- **Tatreez embroidery**, **Dabke dance**, and **oral storytelling** preserved identity.
- **Palestinian Walks**, **Mornings in Jenin**, and **Memory for Forgetfulness** became global texts of resistance.
- Diaspora artists and intellectuals reimagined Palestine through **film**, **music**, and **visual art**.

Debunking Myths

- ❌"Palestinians lost their identity in exile."
  ✅Exile became the forge of modern Palestinian nationalism.
- ❌"The PLO was a terrorist group."
  ✅It evolved into a diplomatic body, recognized by the UN and Arab League.
- ❌"Palestinian culture is static."
  ✅It's dynamic, diasporic, and globally influential.

Chapter 9

The Mirror War—Semitic vs. Semitic in Modern Occupation

Confront the **modern paradox**: a Semitic people occupying another Semitic people.

- Zionism's impact on Arab Jews and Palestinians.
- The ethical crisis of displacement and occupation.
- The world's paralysis in the face of moral clarity.

Zionism's Dual Legacy

Zionism began as a movement for Jewish self-determination in response to centuries of persecution. But its implementation in Palestine created a paradox: a Semitic people seeking refuge displaced another Semitic people already rooted in the land.

- **European Zionism**: Influenced by nationalism and colonialism, it viewed Palestine as a "land without a people" despite its vibrant population.
- **Arab Jews**: Many lived peacefully across the Middle East, but Zionism often erased their identities to fit a European narrative.
- **Palestinian Jews**: Existed before Zionism, but were sidelined in the new state's formation.

"Zionism promised safety—but delivered displacement."

Occupation as Identity Crisis

Israel's occupation of Palestinian land is not just territorial—it's existential.

- **Semitic vs. Semitic**: Jews and Palestinians share linguistic, genetic, and cultural ancestry.
- **Occupation fractures kinship**: It turns cousins into enemies, neighbors into targets.
- **Arab Jews in Israel**: Often marginalized, their Semitic identity diluted by Ashkenazi dominance.

"The occupier and the occupied speak the same ancestral tongue—but cannot hear each other."

Global Paralysis

Despite clear violations of international law, the world remains frozen.

- **UN resolutions ignored**: Over 100 passed against Israeli actions—few enforced.
- **Western complicity**: Arms sales, diplomatic shielding, and media bias sustain the occupation.
- **Selective empathy**: Ukraine's resistance is celebrated; Palestine's is criminalized.

"The world sees Gaza burn—and calls it complicated."

Ethical Collapse

Occupation has eroded moral clarity:

- **Killing civilians is normalized**: Airstrikes on homes, hospitals, and schools met with silence.
- **Humanitarian aid blocked**: Gaza's siege violates Geneva Conventions.
- **Resistance demonized**: Palestinians labeled terrorists for defending their homes.

"When truth is punished, justice becomes treason."

Debunking Myths

- ❌"Israel is the only democracy in the Middle East."
  ✅It denies millions of Palestinians basic rights under military rule.
- ❌"Palestinians teach hate."
  ✅They teach survival under occupation, and resilience in exile.
- ❌"Occupation is security."
  ✅It is control, humiliation, and systemic violence.

Chapter 10

Truth as Resistance—A Call to Conscience

History as a Battlefield

This book has traced the arc of a people erased, renamed, displaced, and demonized. But history is not neutral—it is contested terrain. The occupier rewrites maps, renames cities, and fabricates myths. The resistor reclaims memory, revives language, and resurrects truth.

- **Palestine was never empty.**
- **Palestinians were never foreign.**
- **Resistance was never terrorism.**

"To remember is to resist. To speak truth is to defy empire."

Silence Is Complicity

The world has watched Gaza burn, Jerusalem fragment, and the West Bank suffocate. And yet, silence reigns.

- **Academic institutions** suppress Palestinian voices under the guise of neutrality.
- **Feminist movements** fail to confront colonial violence, betraying their own principles.
- **Religious leaders** offer platitudes while ignoring genocide.
- **Arab states** normalize relations with Israel, abandoning Palestine.

"Neutrality in the face of oppression is not peace—it is betrayal."

Solidarity as Action

Solidarity is not a hashtag. It is not a trend. It is sacrifice, commitment, and confrontation.

- **Boycott, Divestment, Sanctions (BDS)** campaigns have forced corporations and governments to divest.
- **Student encampments** have reignited global resistance.
- **Grassroots movements** have mobilized millions across continents.

"From the river to the sea" is not a slogan—it is a promise of justice.

A Beacon of Resistance

Palestinian resistance is not just local—it is global. It is a mirror for every oppressed people. It is a call to conscience for every silent institution.

- Gaza's endurance has become a symbol of defiance.
- The 2021 Unity Intifada redefined resistance as grassroots, inclusive, and unstoppable.
- The Palestinian struggle is a blueprint for liberation movements worldwide.

Final Myth-Busting

- ❌"Truth is subjective."
  ✅Truth is rooted in lived experience, historical record, and moral clarity.
- ❌"Resistance must be polite."
  ✅Resistance must be effective.
- ❌"Justice is complicated."
  ✅Justice is inconvenient for the powerful—but simple for the oppressed.

Final Words

This book is not a history lesson. It is a weapon. It is a mirror. It is a challenge.

"If you are neutral in situations of injustice, you have chosen the side of the oppressor."

—Desmond Tutu

Let this be a beacon. Let it be a rupture. Let it be a reckoning.

Appendix

Myth-Busting Palestine

A concise, unapologetic appendix designed to dismantle historical distortions. Each myth is met with sharp, verifiable rebuttals.

Section A: **Origins & Identity**

Myth	Truth
"Palestinians are modern Arabs with no ancient ties."	Palestinians trace lineage to Canaanites, Philistines, Jews, and Arameans. DNA studies confirm continuity with Bronze Age Levantines.
"Palestine never existed."	The name *Palestina* was used by Romans from 2nd century CE, adapted from earlier references like *Philistia* in Egyptian and Greek texts.
"Palestinians are recent migrants."	Ottoman records and travelogues show a thriving, diverse population in 18th–19th century Palestine — farmers, merchants, scholars.

Section B: **Colonization & Occupation**

Myth	Truth
"Zionism was peaceful."	Armed militias like Irgun and Haganah carried out massacres, expulsions, and urban warfare. The Nakba was not incidental — it was strategy.
"Israel made the desert bloom."	Palestinian agriculture thrived pre-1948. British reports detail citrus exports, olive groves, and local markets long before Zionist settlement.
"The land was empty."	Palestine had bustling cities — Jaffa, Haifa, Jerusalem — and over 400 villages before 1948.

Section C: **Language & Faith**

Myth	Truth
"All Palestinians are Muslims."	Palestinians include Christians, Druze, and historically, Jews and Samaritans. Christianity predates Islam in Palestine.
"Hebrew and Arabic are unrelated."	Both are Semitic languages, sharing deep linguistic roots and mutual intelligibility in structure.
"Arabic replaced native languages."	Arabic absorbed and evolved from Canaanite, Aramaic, and Syriac roots — it is indigenous to the region's linguistic heritage.

Glossary of Reclaimed Terms

Term	Definition
Semitic	Refers to a family of languages (Hebrew, Arabic, Aramaic) and peoples from the ancient Near East — not a racial category.
Nakba	Arabic for "catastrophe"; refers to the 1948 mass expulsion and destruction of Palestinian society.
Filastin	Arabic term for Palestine, used from early Islamic rule — derived from Latin *Palæstina.*
Tatreez	Traditional Palestinian embroidery, symbol of identity and resistance, often used to record family and village heritage.
Dhimmi	Non-Muslim citizens under Islamic rule granted protection in exchange for a tax — Jews and Christians often lived safely under this system.

Visual Timeline: From Canaan to Occupation

3000 BCE — Canaanite civilization thrives.

1175 BCE — Philistines settle along the southern coast.

1000 BCE — Kingdoms of Israel and Judah emerge.

63 BCE — Roman conquest under Pompey.

70 CE — Second Temple destroyed by Titus.

135 CE — Hadrian renames Judea "Syria Palaestina."

638 CE — Caliph Umar enters Jerusalem peacefully.

1517 CE — Ottoman control begins.

1917 CE — Balfour Declaration issued by Britain.

1947 CE — UN Partition Plan proposed.

1948 CE — Nakba; State of Israel declared.

1964 CE — PLO founded.

1993 CE — Oslo Accords signed.

2023 CE — Gaza under siege; global protests rise.

Bibliograhpy

Absolutely, Mayar — here's a curated **bibliography** to support your book's historical depth, myth-busting clarity, and scholarly integrity. I've grouped sources by theme so you can easily reference them throughout your chapters.

Core Historical Sources

Author	Title	Notes
Walid Khalidi	*All That Remains*	Definitive record of depopulated Palestinian villages in 1948.
Benny Morris	*The Birth of the Palestinian Refugee Problem, 1947–1949*	Israeli historian's archival work on expulsions.
Nur Masalha	*The Palestine Nakba*	Decolonial framing of memory, oral history, and resistance.
Ilan Pappé	*The Ethnic Cleansing of Palestine*	Argues 1948 was a systematic campaign of expulsion.
Rashid Khalidi	*The Hundred Years' War on Palestine*	Traces settler colonialism and resistance from 1917–2017.
Adel Manna	*Nakba and Survival*	Focuses on Palestinians who remained in Haifa and Galilee.

Ancient & Roman-Era Sources

Author	Title	Notes
Flavius Josephus	*The Jewish War*	Eyewitness account of Roman suppression of Jewish revolts.
Karen Armstrong	*Jerusalem: One City, Three Faiths*	Explores religious and historical layers of the city.
Israel Finkelstein & Neil Silberman	*The Bible Unearthed*	Archaeological critique of biblical historicity.
Thomas Asbridge	*The Crusades*	Contextualizes religious conquest and its legacy.

Zionism & Colonialism

Author	Title	Notes
Arthur Hertzberg	*The Zionist Idea*	Anthology of foundational Zionist writings.
Simha Flapan	*The Birth of Israel: Myths and Realities*	Challenges official Israeli narratives.
Lenni Brenner	*The Iron Wall*	Traces Zionist revisionism and its political evolution.
Norman Finkelstein	*Image and Reality of the Israel–Palestine Conflict*	Critical analysis of propaganda and historical distortion.
David Hirst	*The Gun and the Olive Branch*	Investigative history of the conflict.

Cultural & Identity Studies

Author	Title	Notes
Mahmoud Darwish	*Memory for Forgetfulness*	Poetic reflection on exile and resistance.
Ghassan Kanafani	*Palestinian Resistance Literature*	Fiction and essays from a revolutionary voice.
Naim Ateek	*Justice and Only Justice*	Palestinian liberation theology.
Elias Khoury	*Gate of the Sun*	Novel that reconstructs Nakba memory through oral storytelling.

Archival & Reference Works

- Palestine and the Arab-Israeli Conflict: An Annotated Bibliography – Institute for Palestine Studies
- Palestine Remembered Bibliography – Extensive documentation of villages, maps, and statistics
- Oxford Bibliographies: Zionism – Scholarly overview of Zionist historiography
- Palestine (region) - Wikipedia – Etymology, historical transitions, and imperial naming practices

Citation Integration by Chapter

Chapter 1: The Semitic Paradox

[1] Edward Said, *The Question of Palestine* (New York: Vintage Books, 1992), 10–13.
[2] Sami Zubaida, "The Myth of Ethnic Conflict," *Middle East Report* 224 (2002): 4–9.

Chapter 2: Ancient Roots—Pre-Roman Palestine

[1] Israel Finkelstein and Neil Silberman, *The Bible Unearthed: Archaeology's New Vision of Ancient Israel and the Origin of Its Sacred Texts* (New York: Free Press, 2001), 45.
[2] Kathleen Kenyon, *Digging Up Jericho* (London: Ernest Benn, 1957), 29.
[3] DNA studies referenced in Marc Haber et al., "Genome-Wide Diversity in the Levant Reveals Recent Structuring by Culture," *PLoS Genetics* 9, no. 2 (2013).

Chapter 3: Rome's Grip Tightens

[1] Flavius Josephus, *The Jewish War*, trans. G.A. Williamson (London: Penguin Books, 1981), 89–94.
[2] Peter Schäfer, *The History of the Jews in the Greco-Roman World* (New York: Routledge, 2003), 101.

Chapter 4: The Flavian Suppression

[1] Ilan Pappé, *The Forgotten Palestinians* (New Haven: Yale University Press, 2011), 22–23.
[2] Karen Armstrong, *Jerusalem: One City, Three Faiths* (New York: Ballantine Books, 1996), 103.

[3] Hadrian's renaming cited in Michael Grant, *The Twelve Caesars* (New York: Scribner, 1975), 299.

Chapter 5: Byzantine to Islamic Transitions

[1] Fred M. Donner, *The Early Islamic Conquests* (Princeton: Princeton University Press, 1981), 276.
[2] Amikam Elad, "The Conquest of Palestine by the Muslim Arabs," *Jerusalem Studies in Arabic and Islam* 8 (1986): 1–40.
[3] Leila Ahmed, *Women and Gender in Islam* (New Haven: Yale University Press, 1992), 54.

Chapter 6: Ottoman Decline and British Mandate

[1] Rashid Khalidi, *Palestinian Identity: The Construction of Modern National Consciousness* (New York: Columbia University Press, 1997), 116–121.
[2] Walid Khalidi, *Before Their Diaspora* (Washington, D.C.: Institute for Palestine Studies, 1984), 97.
[3] Eugene Rogan, *The Fall of the Ottomans* (New York: Basic Books, 2015), 296.

Chapter 7: The Nakba

[1] Benny Morris, *The Birth of the Palestinian Refugee Problem, 1947–1949* (Cambridge: Cambridge University Press, 1988), 142.
[2] Walid Khalidi, *All That Remains* (Washington, D.C.: Institute for Palestine Studies, 1992), xii.
[3] Avi Shlaim, *The Iron Wall: Israel and the Arab World* (New York: Norton, 2000), 177.

Chapter 8: Exile and Resistance

[1] Mahmoud Darwish, *Memory for Forgetfulness* (Berkeley: University of California Press, 1995), 17.

[2] Ghassan Kanafani, *Men in the Sun and Other Palestinian Stories* (London: Heinemann, 1978), 3–4.
[3] Helena Cobban, *The Palestinian Liberation Organisation: People, Power and Politics* (Cambridge: Cambridge University Press, 1984), 63.

Chapter 9: Semitic vs. Semitic Conflict

[1] Ella Shohat, "Sephardim in Israel: Zionism from the Standpoint of Its Jewish Victims," *Social Text* 19/20 (1988): 1–35.
[2] Norman Finkelstein, *Image and Reality of the Israel–Palestine Conflict* (London: Verso, 2003), 45–50.

Chapter 10: Truth as Resistance

[1] Desmond Tutu, "If You Are Neutral in Situations of Injustice," *The Book of Forgiving*, ed. Mpho Tutu (New York: HarperOne, 2014), 34.
[2] John Pilger, *Freedom Next Time* (London: Bantam Books, 2006), 122.

References

Here's a robust set of **references** to support your book, Mayar — spanning ancient history, colonialism, resistance, and cultural identity. These sources are academically credible, widely cited, and thematically aligned with your chapters.

Historical & Political Foundations

Author	Title	Notes
Edward Said	*The Question of Palestine*	Seminal critique of Zionism and Palestinian erasure.
Rashid Khalidi	*The Hundred Years' War on Palestine*	Frames the conflict as settler colonialism.
Ilan Pappé	*The Ethnic Cleansing of Palestine*	Documents 1948 expulsions and Zionist planning.
Benny Morris	*The Birth of the Palestinian Refugee Problem*	Archival study of Nakba events from Israeli perspective.
Nur Masalha	*The Palestine Nakba*	Focuses on memory, oral history, and decolonization.
David Hirst	*The Gun and the Olive Branch*	Investigative history of Zionism and Western complicity.

Ancient & Roman-Era Sources

Author	Title	Notes
Flavius Josephus	*The Jewish War*	Eyewitness account of Roman suppression.
Karen Armstrong	*Jerusalem: One City,*	Explores religious and

Author	Title	Notes
	Three Faiths	imperial transitions.
Israel Finkelstein & Neil Silberman	*The Bible Unearthed*	Archaeological critique of biblical historicity.

Culture, Identity & Resistance

Author	Title	Notes
Mahmoud Darwish	*Memory for Forgetfulness*	Poetic reflection on exile and siege.
Ghassan Kanafani	*Men in the Sun*	Fictionalized trauma of displacement.
Susan Abulhawa	*Mornings in Jenin*	Multigenerational saga of Palestinian exile.
Raja Shehadeh	*Palestinian Walks*	Memoir of land, loss, and resistance.
Mohammed El-Kurd	*Rifqa*	Contemporary poetry of occupation and defiance.

Reference Lists & Curated Guides

- Middle East Eye's 11 Essential Books — Contextual history and political analysis
- Literary Hub's 40 Books to Understand Palestine — Fiction, memoir, poetry, and resistance
- Five Books Expert Recommendations — Curated by Palestinian and Israeli scholars
- Observer Diplomat's Palestine Reading List — Personal narratives and historical critiques
- The Conversation's Expert Picks — Academic perspectives on Zionism, coexistence, and settler colonialism

Author's Note

Carving Truth in Stone

This book was not born in comfort.

It was carved out of grief, rage, and an undying obligation to memory. I did not set out to write a history book — I set out to write a rupture. To name what has been silenced, to remember what has been erased, and to shout into a world numbed by complicity.

I am not neutral. I do not seek balance between colonizer and colonized. I seek justice. I seek clarity. And I seek a reckoning with the myths that have paralyzed hearts and erased lives.

If you read this and feel uncomfortable — good. History is not a lullaby. It is an alarm. It demands we wake, confront, and act. Especially when oppression wears the mask of security. Especially when silence is sold as diplomacy.

This book is a tribute to the ancient ones who carried this land in their bones. To the refugees who rebuilt identity from ashes. To the poets and revolutionaries who taught the world that exile is not the end — it is the beginning of return.

May this work honor every voice that has been buried, every child who has been lost, and every truth that dares to rise.

Epilogue

We began with keys and silence—with stories folded into exile. Through these pages, we retraced erased names, reopened shuttered doors, and remembered in defiance.

From Nakba's ashes to olive trees scarred by war, this book became a home for every voice that history tried to hush. We lit lamps in corners long darkened, and whispered truths that once trembled.

Now, as the final page turns, we return—not to an ending, but to a promise:
That we will carry the memory.
That we will speak even when told not to.
That silence will not be our inheritance.

To write was to remember.
To read—was to return.

www.ingramcontent.com/pod-product-compliance
Lightning Source LLC
LaVergne TN
LVHW010108110826
845155LV00028B/543

9781915958280